EARTH TONES

To Gilly,
A dear friend and a truly poetical sensitive person...
Regina Merzlak
March 27, 1996

EARTH TONES

Regina Merzlak

☙

Mellen Poetry Press
a division of
Mellen University Press
Lewiston/Queenston/Lampeter/Berlin/Salzburg/Grand Turk

Library of Congress Cataloging-in-Publication Data

Merzlak, Regina.
  Earth tones / Regina Merzlak.
    p. cm.
  ISBN 0-7734-2722-8
  I. Title.
  PS3563.E7462E27 1994
  811'.54--dc20   94-46363
                                                                CIP

Copyright © 1994 Regina Merzlak
All rights reserved. Author inquiries and orders:

Mellen Poetry Press
The Edwin Mellen Press
Box 450
Lewiston, New York 14092

Printed in the United States of America

For Tony and Bart

CONTENTS

Walking in Cambridge	1
The Autumn of Yellow Leaves	2
The Inner World	3
The Sliver Moon	4
Winter Planets	5
Riches	6
The Sunken Path	7
The Bronze Horses of St. Mark's	8
Van Gogh's "*Starry Night*"	10
Journeys	11
Woman of Stone	12
Vignette	13
Wounded	14
Lilacs	15
"Nel' Mezzo del Camin..."	16
The Blue Virgin	17
Angel	18
Apsaras	19
Angel (#2)	20
The House Beneath The Dipper	21
Night Snow	23

Thistles	24
Reflections in a Bear's Eye	26
How the Dark Comes Down	27
Skating on the Marsh	28
Southern Nights	29
Cameos	30
The Touchstone	31
Just as Adonis	32
The Wind	33
The Gift	34
Hidden	35
Myths	36
The Lunch	37
Desires	39
The Brook	40
Praying Mantis	42
Dragonfly	44
The Plum Tree	46
August's End	48
Why Can't I	49
Acknowledgments	50
Author's Note	51

Earth Tones

Walking in Cambridge

Suddenly I turned
The corner and on the downward hill
Saw blue star-flowers in clusters all
Swaying in the chilling wind.
And in my ear the wind had traveled far
The wind had vanquished sound
And I was gone down centuries of space,
One with the flowers, one with the bending pine,
One with this small and winning
Patch of place, blown back like a seed
To the deep ground.

The Autumn of Yellow Leaves

The trees were green for a long time that year.
Summer lingered into mid-November, and it seemed
Everyone turned their heads in great surprise
When no color came, except the occasional red.
But it was not enough to make an autumn in New England.

One day the air began to turn to yellow.
The gingko tree, with its delicate fanned leaf,
Like the Japanese ladies used to hold once
To hide their smiles, was suddenly gilded gold.
The world took on a sunniness, a lemon look.

As I walked the streets, day and dusk,
I could see nothing but yellow, haunting
The dim hours, the shortening days.
It was a premonition, almost a certainty:
Nothing to fear before the end -- only light.

The Inner World

The sweet air of April
Showers golden tree buds
Onto the receiving grass,
        And I am fooled into thinking
        That a south breeze brings
        Warm nights and sunny afternoons.

But the trickster roams always,
Dancing on apple blossoms
And lilacs about to bloom.
        I have gone out too soon
        In flowing dresses,
        And the wind jumps up
        Putting my pale legs to shame.

I shiver and remember that nothing
Comes exactly when and how it should.
So I must wait, whether in light or dark,
For the world that forms itself within,
Speaking a language I have yet to learn.

The Sliver Moon

The sliver moon,
bright in the early night,
dark blue spring night,
(still we shiver in April)
how thin it pencils in
a curve of gold on the
royal sky, a signature
we try to decipher
like fine calligraphy.
Drifting through the dark,
it can only last a day
as do the dearest things --
the delicate sliver moon.

Winter Planets

Like a sword with only handle and point
In perpendicular conjunction
Venus and Jupiter emblazon
The western sky.

But in the myth-time
These lambent orbs led other lives.
Does Venus, brightest of all,
Still seek the ruddy planet,
her partner in love?
Musing on Mars, perhaps, she glows,
Remembering the iron nets
That once upon Olympus
Held them in shackles of desire.

Far below, the white god, in his slower orbit,
Draws out fantasies
Of nymphs and mortal women.

Now in the icy night, I shiver with the stars,
And hesitate to go --
For the sheer beauty of the galaxy,
The incandescent mystery of light.

Riches

How can I take the gold I've hoarded
Over the long dark years,
Thinking it safe to keep it hidden
In the circles of myself,
And breathe it out of me with joy?
Would it go up into the autumn air,
Changed into orange leaves or yellow,
Becoming an oak tree's crown?
And would the sky be bluer
And the leaves more golden
In the integrity of their nature?
And of my nature too, finally,
Not saving the secrets in my soul,
But lavishing them on the world
In this shining rebirth?
Perhaps I might not die, as long as
This place, this planet stays,
As long as I can be transformed
From coins debased, by some other
Alchemy than we know,
To a miraculous reality.

The Sunken Path

You come upon it if you suddenly look down --
The sunken path, I mean -- something pulls you.
You want to look there through the dark green leaves.

A patch of sun trembles on the slate stone,
The way a sad heart would receive a glimmer of hope.
But the long day steals everything away.

Then the old path
Like an old well,
Grows black with sundown.

I look toward the leafy walk once more and wonder
Why on a summer day, it beckons.

The Bronze Horses of St. Mark's

Back in the new world
Beginning-of-summer winds
Dappled by dropping blossoms
Bridal-veil white
Flowers falling on green air
Or apple petals drifting
Over meadows where chestnut
Horses prance and play,

I think of the bronze horses of Saint Mark's
How their old beauty from ancient Greece
Arrived in Byzantium.

But Venice was crazed in that crusade
When centuries later she looted the east
And brought the horses to this now fortunate place.

Their pose of lifted hooves and tilted heads
Gives way to mystery, all in the eyes
That never reflect what they have seen.

Blessed too by God they ride the basilica
Informing the air around them with molten grace
Listening, looking for what is beyond the square.

Perhaps they dream of other lands
Imagining grasses where blossoms fall
Bridal-veil whitening
The summer breeze
Where pastures corral the whirling horses
Not bronze, not stationary
But brown and white and red
Steeds of a young new place
Racing though new mown fields
Under a new world's western sun.

Van Gogh's *"Starry Night"*

He never could have seen that painted sky
Except in dreams. The whirls of light
Explode in circles, drawing in our sight
Until our eyes upon the canvas lie
Throbbing with stars. The tree points high,
The night is sapphire blue and deeply bright.
All is in motion, all has reached its height,
While we can only wonder, only sigh.
He hardly could have seen such shining fire,
The constellations casting out their flame;
But hearts have seen what scarcely can have name,
Created worlds on cloth or golden lyre.
If real or not, we must believe the sight
That made these shapes transform our darker night.

Journeys

And you will float down to the Underworld
              Like a butterfly, Eurydice,
To the places of no return,
              And your yellow fluttering
Keeps alive hope that the Orphean hero
              Your lover, will save you.
More than once he tore through Pluto's realm
              Only to know the final rejection.
Hard to believe music had lost its power;
              Hard to believe the charm of song
Had drowned in the Stygian water's lapping tide.
              O, fixed are the edicts of Fate,
And sooner or later, Eurydice, your youth
              Would fade, no matter the cause,
As you whimper down the tunnels of the black world.

Woman of Stone

> *"Se 'l martiro e dolce..."*
> *Dante*

How could Dante have known she would appear
in his later life, verdant, a metaphor
for all the beauty of nature, a love
so gripping that he tasted only desire?

But she was cold, immobile, a monument
to death, like a statue that keeps silent,
drawing in the soul by its perfected form,
yet only a semblance of reality.

        The closed heart seduces from secret wells
where victims drown whose longing lingers there.

Dante needed to feel the sweetness of suffering.
"Dolce, dolce," as he wrote the lines,
so honeyed with pain that he pictured death
as the ultimate passion and delight.

        We die for what we cannot have.

Vignette

In the early morning
    from my high window
down the dappled shade
    of the street,
I saw her bicycle glide.
    She was one with its motion,
like the gull on its wings
    turning smoothly in the sky above her.

Wounded

Like a sparrow, wing-wounded,
      Who whines his chirp
      Into the darkening air,
I cry out my hurt at my once winged heart.
      That part was broken
      Which let me rise,
And now I can only linger and die.

Lilacs

I did my share of crying
Over you
But the winter is skulking off now
Leaving grey mists of cold
Lingering into March.

The wind is up
Lilac buds recall passion
And if you came out of nowhere
Then why not another?

I did my share of crying
Over you
But now spring beckons
And recalls me from winter dying.
After all
Will this year's lilacs
Nod less gracefully than those
That leaned last year
From long and slender stems?

"Nel' Mezzo del Camin..."

The trees are grey dear
And now that you and I have come this distance
We don't know where to turn
The woods are grey, dear, and moderately cold
No leaf lends cover to hide our confusion
Only the evergreens promise comfort
In the middle of the wood.
I turn to you, for the ground is hard
Where no sun yellows this particular day
And you seem strong
But do you know the place you are
And how much of the wood is left?
I think not.
And yet your eyes provide a sky
From other years.
Looking at their bright and ever outward blue
I stand on tiptoe and kiss your cheek.
You, like the comforter you are
Move your lips to mine.
This way we speak in the middle of the wood
Knowing that however far we have come in
We will go out together.

The Blue Virgin

If I can have any peace
Let me have the peace of your forgetting --
Like the crows that pass through
The blue winds of heaven,
Their black outlines of flight
Now here now gone.
Let us fly from the pain
Inflicted on each other,
Leaving no mark
On the floating sky.
Let us rejoice in laughter,
The resurrection of all tender memories
Filling the consonant air with music.
Let me hear music from your soul
Mixed with words of kindness,
And let there be remembering
In the eyes' sight
Of planets blazing down
On the city statue of a blue Virgin,
Her arms outstretched forever
In the peace of all forgetting.

Angel

Angel, now in March of the year
As winter dies on frozen ground
Why do you torment me?

I feel in my knees the whip of your wings
As I walk in branched paths
Hearing you hiss in my ears ceaselessly.

Yet you are my guardian, Angel,
All the days of my life
And if you push me out of winter
Harshly into spring light
I think you know how death
Gives way to birth.

So I accept your assault
Your quick surprising slap,
And your playful spirit

Doing cartwheels on my shoulder,
While guiding me with strictest hand
The very strictest measure of love.

Apsaras
    (Buddhist Angels)

                                  For James Winfield

There is delight in the different:
To see carved in stone
On the ceiling of Buddhist caves
Angels of the far east kingdom
Trailing unfamiliar wings
In an imagined air.

They grin or frown, letting us know
There is no surprise in their unique
Extensions like long flames where they fly.
What, after all, is the Renaissance to them,
The golden-haired seraphs, the double-feathered wings,
The beatific smiles on rounded faces?

In a supple world the helper has many forms
But always is suppliant to the spirit.
Angels, east or west, I think, whatever shapes
They choose, are always arriving, always coming
To try what they can do to ease our crossings.
Apsaras of the long wings, do not forget me,
For though you are strange, I recognize you,
And I love you, taking delight in the different.

Angel (#2)

O pure spirit, of neither gender made,
I think of your beauty, all necessity
Of mingling done away, integrity innate,
Bodiless being without thought for self,
Messenger for the Divine, and harbinger
Of good to man. If only we ask.

I have often seen white about me flutter,
Quick hands touching, experienced
In sweet preoccupation of my need.
For I know you, angel, you mine alone,
But others too moving about me,
Over my head, casting shadows of light.

I hear your voice in the dead silence
Of my ear, and once I saw you all --
Winged battalions in the deep blue sky,
Flying on orange clouds of afterglow.
For you are everywhere, being on being,
Unseen epiphany of another order,
Ordered to lighten our darker sphere.

The House Beneath The Dipper

At four in the morning
I awoke to the world
Outside my window. It displayed
The sprawling Dipper, bright
As hanging gems over my head.

To see that childhood constellation
Spread in giant proportions high above me,
Scooping the air with its spoon's handle,
Brought back the deep delight of younger years,
When eyes were filled with innocent surprise
That so wonderful a shape could hang
Without careening downward to the earth.

Night Snow

Now in the deepest time of night
Sleep is covered with a pure blanket
        of snow.
No sound wakes me as I dream
Of the far reaches of childhood joy.
        The whistle
Of a late train cannot break the peace
That enacts the play of other years
        when we
Were young. In those ecstatic moments
We shaped white drifts into angel wings,
        and flakes
Became ice balls carrying our shouts to the sky.
Those shouts cannot wake us on this winter night,
        for we
Are protected snow deep in an unconscious world
Where delighted images of our youngest years
        cannot die.

Thistles

The purple thistle
    hung down
As I had left it in the field --
    a failed hope
Of stealing away the majestic flower
    without rival.
I had wandered far that day,
    ploughing through
Tall grasses summer-greened.

It was the wild thistle
    I was after,
In the deep gold afternoon.
    I stood there,
The meadow stretching away,
    alone.
A stillness dropped down
    as if I had died
And was reborn from silence
    outside of time.

Emptiness told me something
    about nature.
Its treasures could not be stolen,
    were untouchable
As dreams, real as myth.
    Yet purple thistles
Bloomed everywhere, holding regal heads
    in the blurred air,
Beckoning to me in the quiet hush.

    So I broke the stalk,
Pricking my hand to blood and
    dropped the flower.
Clouds huddled to shade.
    The silence snapped
Into sound, the sun fled,
    and I fled too
Without the blossom rich and rare,
    without the prize.

Reflections in a Bear's Eye

The dark eye of a black bear
Carries the forest trees in its depth,
Reflects the mahogany air with bright
Occasional sundrops, mirrors the cave
Where it was born, moves with ripples
Of shining streams, sees the black earth rising
Upward where he walks through ancestral paths.

Nothing in the thick woods
Is so alive as his hunting look,
His instinctual force, the piercing secret
Of his eyes' search, the unconscious sight
From centuries past, lonely and brutal,
But often harmless, in the wild arboreal dark.

How the Dark Comes Down

How the dark comes down
Is from the bottom up.
The grass and stubble fields
Are already dark below
Before the dark comes down.

Slowly, how slowly, does the lack of light
Settle the earth
So that we do not despair.

In all this blackened world,
The eyes of stars, the face of yellow moons
Scatter enough of light
To push away the primal fear that lurks
When the dark comes down.

Skating on the Marsh

Dark ice on the marsh,
Barely lit by the moon
Yet somehow better than day.
Was it the tree twig
That frightened our eyes,
Making a scream rise up
Into the black and startled air?
Or was it the danger
Of gleaming water in the night
Propelling our sharpened blades away?
Stay to the center! Stay to the center!
(But the thrill was at the edge.)

There was never anything quite like
The odd and rough and beautiful
Skating on the marsh.

Southern Nights

If I could live until a great old age
        It would be here
Breathing in the balm and breeze
        Of southern nights.

They come on quickly, after the sun
        Darkens this place of oranges,
Softer than air that closes the sea
        Down to its inky black.

Southern nights have made me beautiful
        In ways that defy the mirror.
My long white skirts billow in the black
        And my skin is cool though copper.

Raising my eyes to the spangled skies
        I see the constellation of Orion
Buckling the void with his three-star belt,
        While Venus blazes in the west.

I live the myths I see. In this warm world
        Joy pours down into lungs and eyes
And I am steeped in mystery unveiled
        And southern nights I love.

Cameos

Resting softly on red chalcedony,
White layers carve themselves
Into an artful face that lives and breathes
Through clouded molecules of matter.
Shapes delineate, letting parts dissolve
From the substance of the face rising
Out of its matrix. And when you said
You saw me that way, as a cameo,
I wonder if you meant I seemed well-set
Against a background. Or was it someone
Returned in time from long ago to now?
Do I, for you, never escape the material
From which I came, or do you suppose
I am enshrined and always kept apart?

I like to think you mean that cameos
Are something precious, as in themselves alone,
Each one, one of a kind, showing the noble part,
And that you see behind the face a deeper source
For the fathomless eyes and smile
Worked by an artisan who knew the Antique well.

For Naples is an old place, and the most
Beloved cameos are wrought in the sun.
Yet somehow I hope this gem offers my self
To you as something comforting and serene,
And always is for you a relic that protects
The beauty carved in your own jeweled heart,
Your own sharp-faceted jeweled mind.

The Touchstone

Then I came to the room which filled your days
Asking for wisdom about many things
Hoping to pierce the blue wave of your eye
The wall against which I had crushed my heart.
Ah, no more the light of love
Only the wary look and the forced smile
The stone defense against my silent plea.
All courtesy, civility, you and I
Like boats that foundered long ago in a warm sea
Resting their skeletons now side by side
Taking but little comfort in the same wreckage.
Where was the touchstone I should have used
To measure gold in you?

Just as Adonis

O how I miss you
    How my days go down
    Into tunnels of airlessness
    Or winds that whistle in the dark
    And the days that end in golden glory
    On the tops of trees
    Lose their life since you are gone.

Just as Adonis
    By his beauty brought
    All things to splendor
    You lighted the world
    Wherever I used to walk
    So that I sped through space
    With the winged feet of gods.

Now you are gone
    Though they say you are here
    Still you are invisible to me
    As the electric shock
    That once ran between us
    And now has blown its power
    So that even a memory has no spark.

The Wind

The wind has whipped branches into brooms,
Swept out the sky,
Discovered stars.
They too sway with the trees,
Their glitter moves with the boughs
And one sits now in a corner of my window pane,
Now in another.

Just so you have swept clean my heart,
Left it an empty space,
Then dropped the star
Of your love like fire
Which flares out in passion,
In pain, now here at one point,
Now at another in my being.

The Gift

Whatever is learned young is learned forever
No matter later sight or richer tongue.
It is the old deep memory that never
Betrays the truth or leaves the vision hung
Upon the air to cloud a newer day.
The stream that silvered underneath the moon
Of summer nights, and like a serpent lay,
Is still the mystery that leads to ruin.

Nor do we ever lose the early sight
Of those immortal revels of the sun,
When we were taken up into the light
To be with wind and trees and grasses one.
So death and hope remain, and of these two
I choose the sum of hope to give to you.

Hidden

If I could love you freely, without fear
How would it be in this well-tempered world
Where suns must rise on time and set the same
And my heart's excess would be given blame?
If I could love you freely, O my dear
What foolish fashions would my heart unfurl
Knowing no reason why this passion came
Nor how to root it out and end the game.
But each day that I see you I am burned
And there can be no cure, no help be learned.
I love your self and therefore such excess
Is better hidden than so free expressed.
Thus I alone know how I truly love
While others think as friends we mostly move.

Myths

In the early night I miss you
When I walk in the black air,
And maple buds swell
With unscented perfume.

Then I look up at the sky
Searching among the spangled stars
For your divine election
Placed above all other persons
In my hidden heart.

You are not there among the planets.
They silently glow red and white
And yellow. Only the constellations
Speak out old myths and lift away
The pain in my floating eyes.

The Lunch

We swept through universes
    In a small cucina
Where the cooking flavors
    Mingled with our words.

To think that revelations
    Lived there for a while
From love to angst to laughter
    As light glowed all around.

When lunch-time rush was over
    The small cucina closed
We moved our metaphysics
    To your white waiting car.

Then poetry took over
    And as my poems flew by
Through your long searching fingers
    And your illumined eye,

I judged the word "quintessence"
    To be of greater worth
As you became the touchstone
    That rubbed my words to gold.

We sat there as the rain fell;
    The car was full of light,
And the spirit of our silence
    Kept the ghosts away that night.

Desires

In my desire for the dazzling glance
I have forgotten many subtle things
The sweet screech of the nighthawk's voice
Flying above me in the city street
Piercing the cool of the summer dusk.

In my desire for the cunning word
I have forgotten many common things
The simple speech of the scolding squirrel
The noisy sparrow in the old oak tree
Waiting for seasons to come and go.

In my desire for the passion and the play
I have forgotten many dearer things
The orange cloud at sunset's falling
The heart's faith in a single love
Hoping that it will outlive death.

The Brook

In the recent dark
The bright moon lit the fields.
But in the deep grove
Covered with trees
Darkness lay thick and palpable.
It was here the brook held sway
In the middle of the dark.
It was mysterious
Because it moved in a motionless place.
It was fearsome
Because it showed itself rarely
When the moon made it silver.
Standing under the trees
I watched its sinuosity
And thought of snakes.
Yet the brook was a little thing
Starting from a spring
In the cow pastures and flowing through acres
Into a small stream or inconsequential river.
I stared and stared.
It is hard to leave nature
So beautiful and deadly at the same time.

I was enticed to stay
To feel the winding of the brook
Silver-black, silver-black
Standing in the only waking dream I ever had.
But the stars were sliding toward morning
And the brook was sliding toward its end.
Slowly I went away while in my heart
There remained a longing
For something I could not understand.
Under the dark trees a flash of silver water
Saluted my going.
It was, I think, a warning.

Praying Mantis

There is nothing like the benediction of nature,
When a willow leaf falls early into your lap,
Yellow, some kind of reminder of autumn days,
Or a butterfly brushes your face softly,
Stroking away tears not yet shed.
Yet among these blessed things may come
Surprises, as you sit totally unaware
Beside the blue pool splashing with children's laughter.
Something green will hit your arm, and jumping away,
You turn in fright to see the praying mantis
Standing in the remembered position
Of all your schoolbooks and your dreams.
Praying it is, which seems to redeem the atavistic dread,
Begging with tiny hands to be something other
Than it is, to be a companion to our humanity,
A part of our summer world of sun and water.

Earth Tones

Condemned to a fate of eating the fathers
Of its children, its greenness now
Signals the sweet and virginal creature
It still remains, linked forever to us
By some instinctual preference for the pure.
Nor can we gloat, we who have eaten
Half our world, with not so much
As a prayer, not so much as a putting together
Of hands, as this giant insect does.
To our eyes it seems bizarre, yet we must love
This outward expression of our inward selves,
Not knowing how we appear to other beings,
But hoping to stay with them for a little while.

Dragonfly

Yes, the blue dragonfly
Of all our childhoods
Still beats the summer air
To stillness.
In the shaded brook
Where the black snake sleeps
At high noon,
And the green weeds
Make shelter and smell,
The blue dragonfly
Threads together lightly
The fragile dream.

Wait for the shadows
In the brook to reassemble,
For the stone to show its mica to the sun.
Will the small fish rest in secret sanctuary
Beneath the rock?
Will the jewel-weed turn to silver under water?
The world is a perennial hope of gods and alchemists.
Wait until another day forms itself
Behind the setting sun.

Yes, the blue dragonfly
Darts here
Darts there
With wings unseen
But blue body bright
In the summer light.
From what universe
Does it descend time without end
To thread together lightly
The fragile dream?

The Plum Tree

My father never thought
(though he believed)
that the small plum tree
he planted in the field
would ever purple its stems
with fruit.

       Still, every summer
evening my sister and I
would follow my father
around the meadow examining
the fruit trees. Cherries were good
if you picked them before the birds.
Apples always blushed to red,
and pears made a small appearance.
But the plum tree stayed green.

Earth Tones

One night toward the end of summer,
on our usual tour,
my sister and I saw our father
standing in front of the plum tree.
"Come here and see" he whispered.
We followed his eyes
to a purple globe hanging there:
blue and dusky-red and purple.
"I never thought" he mused,
"it would grow this far north."

        Would we pick it now and eat it?
No, not for a while, not for a while.
We guessed it was a monument to hope.

August's End

There were many signs to search for.
At the pool for instance
the air cooled on August's final days.
But the sun remained as bright
as lemons and hot as fire.
Still the pool picked up the air
Making our bodies shiver just a little.

The long-lasting black-eyed susans
began to disappear, and at night
the gigantic Dipper seemed to tip itself
onto a lower horizon. Meteors fell.

You could smell the sweet decay,
definite death looking like life,
vestigial days so beautiful
with bright confusion that the heart
leaped up this one more time
before it must admit that summer
was gone, and with it the lingering traces
that floated, short-lived, on dreams.

Why Can't I

Why can't I
With clear eye and contented mind
Accept the world?
But I was twice born already.

The first time from the flesh,
        in the green tree
        the summer-murmuring bee
        the white and burning star.

And then again, in the person of those
        who sang ageless songs.
        "nature the gentlest mother is..."
        "A thing of beauty is a joy for ever..."

Why can't I
In softer shadows lie?
There, in some older place
I could perhaps keep pace,
But not as now, lose my soul
To the meager dole which this world
Feeds me through random dreams.

ACKNOWLEDGMENTS

"Angel"   appeared in *Spirit*, Spring/Summer 1991.
                    Copyright Seton Hall University.

"Apsaras"   appeared in *Spirit*, Spring/Summer 1991.
                    Copyright Seton Hall University.

"Angel (#2)"   appeared in *Spirit*, Spring/Summer 1991.
                    Copyright Seton Hall University.

"Night Snow"   appeared in *Spirit*, Volume 58, 1993.
                    Copyright Seton Hall University.

"Myths"   appeared in *Spirit*, Volume 58, 1993.
                    Copyright Seton Hall University.

Author's Note

Regina Merzlak was born in Waterbury, Connecticut, and is a Lecturer in Classics and Mythology at Tufts University in Medford, Massachusetts. She published a book of collected poems, UNDERLIGHT, with the Mellen Poetry Press in 1993.